Welsh long-houses

Four centuries of farming
at Cilewent

The long-house of Cilewent re-erected at the Welsh Folk Museum.

Welsh Long-houses

Four centuries of farming at Cilewent

EURWYN WILIAM

UNIVERSITY OF WALES PRESS
NATIONAL MUSEUM OF WALES

CARDIFF
1992

First published 1992
© University of Wales Press and the National Museum
of Wales

British Library Cataloguing in Publication Data

A catalogue record for this book is available from the
British Library

ISBN 0–7083–1164–4

Front cover:
Cilewent long-house, Welsh Folk Museum, St Fagans

Back cover:
Cilewent long-house: the interior

Cover photographs by A.G. Holland
Cover design by Pica, Cardiff

Typeset in 10pt Baskerville by Afal, Cardiff
Printed in Wales by Qualitex Printing Limited

Introduction

The buildings best preserved over the centuries have normally been the homes of the rich and powerful. Proportionately, they have survived in greater numbers than the often temporary constructions of inferior materials occupied by the majority of our ancestors. Yet many seemingly unremarkable agricultural buildings – adapted and perhaps rebuilt once or twice in their history, but still in use today – have their origins in the primitive farming practices of northern Europe. In fact, they are a link in a tradition that dates back to the Bronze Age.

The long-house – a farmhouse which gave warmth and shelter to people and animals under one roof – was common throughout the British Isles in the fourteenth and fifteenth centuries. Eventually more sophisticated expectations of living conditions in the English lowlands led to the construction of detached farmhouses with outbuildings for the animals. However, in the poorer, upland areas the old ways persisted and long-houses continued to be built up until the early nineteenth century. In Wales, Ireland and the Highlands and Islands of Scotland a diminishing number of long-houses still retained their original functions as home for farmer and animals at the beginning of the twentieth century.

This book traces the origins and development of the long-house in Wales. It also takes a closer look at one particular farmhouse – Cilewent – originally from mid-Wales but now reconstructed at the Welsh Folk Museum, St Fagans, Cardiff. Cilewent was donated to the museum by its owners, Birmingham Corporation, in 1955; work began on re-erecting it in 1957 and it was opened to the public in 1959. Through the documentation, maps and records unearthed for Cilewent farm, the meticulous research undertaken during the reconstruction, and an analysis of building methods, we are able to piece together a vivid mosaic of Welsh rural life over almost five centuries.

The origins of the long-house

Buildings in which a farmer and his cattle lived together under a common roof have a long tradition on the European mainland, a tradition dating back as far as the Bronze Age. The many excavated examples in Denmark, Norway and Sweden show that this was the characteristic house plan in Scandinavia during the Iron Age and Viking periods, and was exported from thence to Ireland, Greenland and the Northern Isles of Britain. Apart from Mawgan Porth in Cornwall, where a dry-stone building probably of the tenth century AD showed clear evidence for division into two parts, one for the humans and one for the animals, long-houses do not appear in the English archaeological record until the thirteenth century. Excavations on two sites at Hound Tor in Dartmoor and on other sites at Hutholes and Beere in Devon, and Old Lanyon in Cornwall and on Fyfield Down in Wiltshire have revealed long-houses with dry-stone walls of this date. These houses had a fire in the centre of the floor in the living portion, and clear evidence for cattle in the lower half, in the form of stone mangers, posts for cow-ties, and stone-lined drains. The two halves were usually divided by a cross-passage formed by two opposing doors but were not otherwise physically separated.

Long-houses of similar form, but of later date, are known from many sites in England, such as Upton in Gloucestershire, West Hartburn in Co. Durham, Wharram Percy in Yorkshire, Riseholme in Lincolnshire, West Whelpington in Northumberland, Wythemail in Northamptonshire, and Hangleton in Sussex. Some are of the fourteenth and fifteenth centuries: those at West Whelpington may be as late as the seventeenth century in date. The distribution of medieval long-houses in England is widespread, except for parts of the Midlands, Kent and East Anglia. These archaeological traces are strengthened by documentary references such as the 'unam domum pro aula sua et pro bovaria sua' (a house with its hall and cow quarters) recorded in Worcestershire in 1408. Nevertheless, it is clear that over most of lowland England the long-house had disappeared by the middle of the sixteenth century; at Gomeldon in Wiltshire the change-over from a long-house to a detached house and buildings happened as early as the thirteenth century.

The very early and primitive long-houses are known only from excavations. The improved long-house which replaced them still survives in many cases. These were also mainly of one storey and had an open hearth with no structural division between the hall and byre, but they were substantially built with heavy timber cruck trusses holding up the roof. There is a group of such houses in north Yorkshire and Cumberland. The first large and consistent group of English long-houses to survive, however, appear in Devon towards the middle of the sixteenth century, and are of substantial stone construction. The fire in its central open hearth has been replaced by a chimney set against the cross-passage, so that the house is physically divided from the byre by the chimney-stack. In those cases where the stack is set in a side wall, the two parts are separated by a stone wall or a stout timber partition. These houses continued to be built until the late seventeenth century: from then on they began to be adapted to serve different needs.

In Cumberland and Westmorland the classic long-house was common in the late seventeenth century, with a heavy concentration of building between 1680 and 1710. They are more uniform in plan and more commodious than those in Devon, but by the late eighteenth century, they too were starting to become outdated. In Scotland, it is clear that before the eighteenth century long-houses were as common in the Lowlands as they were in the Highlands. Certainly farmhouses of this type were being erected in the Highlands around 1800, and in the Outer Hebrides several can still be found fulfilling their original function. The 'black houses' of the Hebrides are a specialized form, with a porch and barn attached to

Cwmeilath, Llansadwrn, Dyfed. The front of the house is painted pink while all the other walls are white. The cowhouse includes a dairy. As it stands it is an addition to the house: there is a straight joint at the front and its rear wall is set back from the house. The house includes scarfed cruck trusses, in contrast to the later collar-beam trusses of the cowhouse. The farm was of 85 acres in 1896 and kept eight milking cows, ten other cattle, three horses and five sheep. (This is one of a series of photographs taken for David Jenkins, an architect of Llandeilo, in 1896.)

the basic long-house unit. In Ireland too, long-houses were common, especially in the north-west, until the twentieth century.

Various theories have been put forward to explain the origins of the long-house. One school of thought has seen it as a manifestation of the Celtic lands, ignoring the fact that long-houses were common in both Bronze Age Central Europe and in Dark Age Scandinavia. Another school of thought sees it as a normal response to the problem of housing both man and beast at the least possible expense and inconvenience, and as such likely to be found in every culture at some stage of its development. One of the most modern explanations combines both social and climatic factors. Long-houses appear to have become common in Britain in the thirteenth century, when the economic growth of the peasantry coincided with a climatic deterioration. An increasing number of cattle

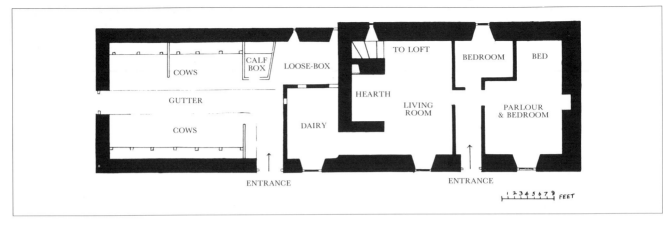

COWS

CALF
BOX

LOOSE-BOX

TO LOFT

BEDROOM

BED

GUTTER

HEARTH

COWS

DAIRY

LIVING
ROOM

PARLOUR
& BEDROOM

ENTRANCE

ENTRANCE

1 2 3 4 5 6 7 8 9 FEET

Plan of Cwmeilath farmhouse drawn by Iorwerth C. Peate (first Curator of the Welsh Folk Museum) in 1936.

Rear view of Cwmeilath farmhouse, Llansadwrn, Dyfed, 1896.

thus had to be wintered indoors, both for their own good and to protect the fields from their treading, as well as to conserve bedding. In the arable areas where long-houses were absent, bedding straw was available in plenty for the local practice of wintering the cattle in open yards. Very early on, however, fashion began to dictate that the animals should be separated from the humans, and so before the middle of the sixteenth century the long-house had been replaced by a farmhouse and detached buildings over most of lowland England. Only in the possibly less sophisticated areas of the west and north, with their different agricultural emphasis, did the long-house idea survive.

Early long-houses in Wales

Possibly the earliest testimony regarding the existence of long-houses in Wales is neither archaeological nor architectural, but documentary. *The Dream of Rhonabwy* is one of the series of tales together known as *Y Mabinogi*: it appears to have been composed in Powys in the thirteenth century. It includes a fairly lengthy description of the hall of Heilyn Goch which must be a long-house, noting the entry of Rhonabwy and his companions into what was clearly the cowhouse-end and progressing thence to the hall:

And as they came towards the house, they could see a black old hall with a straight gable end, and smoke a-plenty from it. And when they came inside, they could see a floor full of holes and uneven. Where there was a bump on it, it was with difficulty a man might stand thereon, so exceeding slippery was the floors with cows' urine and their dung. Where there was a hole, a man would go over the ankle, what with the mixture of water and cow-dung; and branches of holly a-plenty on the floor after the cattle had eaten off their tips. And when they came to the main floor of the house they could see bare dusty dais boards, and a crone feeding a fire on the one dais, and when cold came upon her she would throw a lapful of husks on to the fire, so it was not easy for any man alive to endure that smoke ...

The *Dream of Rhonabwy* contains many elements of satire and it has been recently suggested that this description is also satirical, and that Heilyn Goch's hall would never have looked like this. This could well be so; but nevertheless it seems clear that the author has based his description on scenes that were familiar to him.

We cannot say with any certainty what a typical medieval farmhouse in Wales looked like, for only a very few of the best examples have survived. The earlier the period the smaller the chance of survival. There is a considerable element of chance in what will or will not endure, but certainly one of the major factors is how well-built a structure originally was. The most solidly constructed houses were the homes of the wealthiest people, and so it is that throughout history we know more about their homes and way of life than about the daily circumstances of their poorer neighbours. Medieval castles have commonly survived, but few Welsh cottages are older than two centuries, for the poor could not afford building materials that would last. The poorer farmhouses and the small crofts of the Middle Ages have all disappeared without trace, and it is only in south-east Wales that their remains are beginning to be unearthed through excavation.

Of those medieval houses that have stood the test of time, however, it seems that the hall-house, a large and occasionally ornate single-storey structure open to the roof, was a popular type. The plan of this, like houses of similar date elsewhere in Britain, consisted of a large room, the hall, with a through-passage at its lower end screened off from a lesser room or rooms. The latter were most commonly service rooms, namely kitchen, buttery or pantry. There was usually a loft over them, as over the parlour if there was one beyond the upper or dais end of the hall. In mid-Wales the passage partition often has open panels, as at Tŷ Mawr, Castell Caereinion (not infilled with wattle as was more normal), supporting the view that the lower end in such cases might have been a byre. While it is clear that the very best hall-houses were not long-houses, it seems equally likely that their poorer contemporaries, which have not survived, did indeed have cattle housed in their lower ends. A small late medieval hall-house on the Powys–Clwyd border, for example, Cil-eos Isaf, Pennant, was certainly a long-house.

Poorer long-houses would have been long, low buildings, their roofs of thatch and their walls of timber or perhaps clay. They were sited on a slope, with the upper end dug out of the slope and the earth thrown further down to form a platform for the lower end. The animals were housed at this end so that the

Ystradaman, Betws, Dyfed, taken in 1896. A seventeenth-century house to which the cowhouse was added in the late nineteenth century. There is no trace of an earlier roof-line on the gable, but the old entrance through the gable remains in use. The door to the feeding-passage is treated as part of the house.

manure could be disposed of more easily. Inside, there was only one room, with two doors (usually) facing each other forming a central cross-passage. We know nothing about the internal arrangements of these houses, but we can imagine an open fireplace on the floor, with the smoke filling the roof-space. Its only

means of escape was through the windows, which were placed opposite one another: since they were not glazed, one had to be closed in the wind and rain, light being admitted through the opposite window. The family slept on a platform set slightly higher than the floor. It was an old tradition in the Celtic countries

Farmhouse and cowhouse at Ystradaman, 1896.

that cows would produce more milk if they could see the flames of the fire. This belief persisted in Radnorshire (where the Cilewent long-house came from) until this century. Beyond this belief was an even older one, the belief in the power of fire to protect the animals from evil spirits and other ills.

Regional farmhouse types

In the late sixteenth century we begin to see various distinctive regional house-plans in Wales. They continued to provide the standard type of farmhouse dwelling in the country until a uniform centrally planned type of house began to be created under the influence of Georgian pattern-books in the early eighteenth century. These new houses differed from the hall-house in that they were of two storeys, with a staircase and a permanent fireplace. Many of the lofts appear to have been used for the storage of farm produce such as seed corn: for many years, therefore, the ground floor continued in use as a sleeping area.

There seem to have been four main regional types of farmhouse in Wales, each type concentrated in a core-area but often with a considerable number of outlying examples in other regions. The predominant sub-medieval house in north-west Wales was entered through a cross-passage some two-thirds of the way along its length, this passage forming the lower end of the main room or hall. The fireplace was at the far or upper end of the hall, against the gable, while the space below the passage was usually partitioned to form two small rooms. This type of house also exists in considerable numbers in south-east Wales.

The predominant type in north-east Wales also had its doorways in this position, but the fireplace was sited not at the upper end of the hall but on one of its side walls. This is probably the earliest type of enclosed fireplace found in Wales, for it appears in the last generation of open-hall houses as well as in the earliest dated storeyed houses. Several of these houses are also found in north-west Wales; there is a considerable number of them in the south-east; and they cluster around the Pembrokeshire coast. The commonest house type in the old mid-Wales counties of

The doorway of Esgair farmhouse, Llansadwrn, Dyfed, 1896. A long, low structure throughout, though the ridge of the cowhouse is lower than that of the house and the cowhouse is a markedly narrower structure. The only entry to the house is through the passage, which, however, has had a dairy inserted into its far end. David Jenkins noted, 'I much wondered to see the old oak door and frame working now as of old, in its peg and hole; the tenants must be well using them, or they could never last; this door cannot be less than 200 years old.' The farm was of 60 acres in 1896, with six cows, four other cattle, two horses and two sheep.

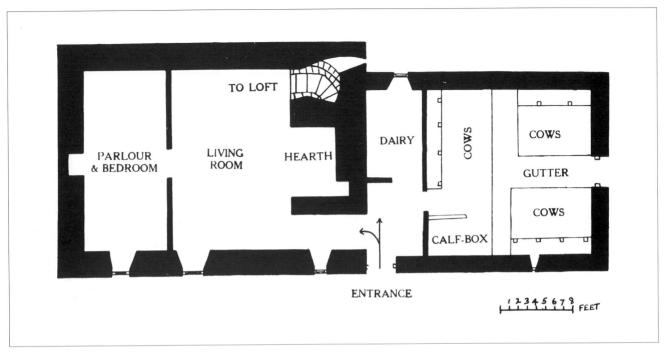

Montgomeryshire and Radnorshire (north and mid Powys), on the other hand, had the chimney so sited that the side of the fireplace faced the entry, so that a small lobby took the place of the cross-passage. A variant of this type occurs commonly in Glamorgan: this has a second stack on a gable wall, a position more like that found in the rest of Wales. Several examples of this type of house are also found in Clwyd.

The commonest type of plan in south-east Wales is based on the entrance being in the gable next to the main fireplace. A one-room house of this type, or one that had a parlour at the upper end of the house, was thus entered directly through the gable and past the side of the fireplace. Many examples had a room at the lower end of the house with a cross-passage located along the length of the building. This room was

Ty'r Celyn, Llandeilo, Dyfed – a photograph taken in 1896. A structure of classic long-house form but of two builds, with the cowhouse being added later. A lean-to cart-shed with wattle walls and a thatched roof has been built against the gable of the house. Ty'r Celyn was a farm of 88 acres on which nineteen cattle, horses and fourteen sheep were kept in 1896.

sometimes used as a byre, forming a long-house. The main fireplace of the hall was not at the upper end but rather backing on to the cross-passage, so that anyone entering the hall had to make a right-angled turn past the side of the fireplace. This type of house can thus be easily recognized from the outside, for it had the door immediately to one side of the main chimney stack. The room at the lower end is often an addition to the main part of the house. This type of house continued to be built up to the middle of the eighteenth century but by that time other, more classical, plan-forms were rapidly gaining ground. This

Another view of Ty'r Celyn from the front (1896).

group of plans is ubiquitous in Gwent, the Glamorgans, southern Powys (the old Breconshire) and parts of Dyfed (north-east Carmarthenshire and most of Cardiganshire) with scattered examples elsewhere in mid and north Wales.

These are also the areas where the vast majority of Welsh long-houses have been recorded. The earliest surviving long-houses come from south-east Wales and date from the seventeenth century, though this date is determined more by the availability of the surviving

evidence than anything else: the seventeenth century is the period from which farmhouses in general have survived in large numbers in eastern Wales. A small number of excavated long-houses is known, however, from some of the deserted medieval villages of Glamorgan, namely Porthceri, Merthyr Dyfan and Barry, the last site yielding several examples of the thirteenth and fourteenth centuries. In western Wales, on the other hand, most farmhouses date from the eighteenth or even the nineteenth centuries, and little

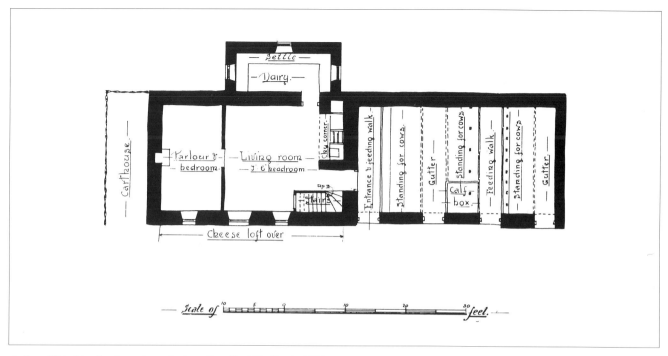

Settle

Dairy

Parlour & bedroom

Living room 9'6' headroom

Chy corner

Entrance & feeding walk

Standing for cows

Gutter

Standing for cows

Feeding walk

Standing for cows

Gutter

Calf box

Carthouse

up

Cheese loft over

— Scale of feet.

A plan of Ty'r Celyn farmhouse drawn by the architect David Jenkins in 1896.

excavation has been carried out, so early evidence is correspondingly scarcer. Remarkably few long-houses are known from north Wales, though it must be presumed that they were formerly more common there also. A document of 1607 makes it clear that long-houses were known in the Machynlleth area, as several witnesses testified to their practice of going in the night to look at their cattle tied up 'in the lower end of the house'. A seventeenth-century report regarding Dyserth in Clwyd mentions that in certain houses 'man and beast have ever lived under the same roofe'.

Left: *A view of Ty'r Celyn in the 1960s. This shows the structural changes made forty years earlier when the house was raised to two storeys, the old gable entrance blocked and a new central doorway formed.*

13

Nevertheless, the distribution of the gable-entry house is essentially the same as that of the long-house in Wales, and has given rise to one of the main debates concerning the origin of the long-house: is the long-house a gable-entry house with a cowhouse added at a later date (and so, since these regional plan types only become common in the seventeenth century, a fairly late manifestation), or is the gable-entry house a long-house shorn of its byre, or at least the vestigial remains of such a tradition? A partial answer, at least, can be obtained by looking very briefly at the houses of Gwent.

GWENT

Gwent (or Monmouthshire as it used to be called) is firmly within the culture-province of the gable-entry house: its normal farmhouse has a cross-passage leading directly to an outer room and, past the back of the fireplace, to the hall. Sir Cyril Fox and Lord Raglan in their great work on the houses of the county regarded the long-house as one of the two cultural strands which combined to produce the typical plan of their late-sixteenth century farmhouse, the other strand being derived from the lowland hall-house. The outer room seems to have been used for a variety of purposes: it would have been a kitchen, buttery or pantry; more commonly, it was used as a parlour, sometimes with a cellar beneath it; and in some instances it was clearly used as a cowhouse, in a classical long-house arrangement. Only half-a-dozen long-houses of one build, that is with the house and cowhouse clearly of the same date, were examined by Fox and Raglan: of these several had exceptionally wide cross-passages, of 9 feet (2.7m) at both Dan-y-bwlch, Bwlch Trewyn and Upper Hafod-arthen, Llanhilleth, for example. This very wide cross-passage has been seen in other houses, where the outer room was originally a cowhouse entered through the common door of the cross-passage. This wide cross-passage is thought to have been necessary for the cattle to turn into the cowhouse since they cannot bend their backbones from side to side.

Although only half-a-dozen long-houses of one build are known from Gwent, far more houses are known which could conform to this pattern were the outer room not an addition, whether it be kitchen, parlour or cowhouse. In some instances of this type the cross-passage is again of considerable width. Fox and Raglan suggested that this addition was no more than a rebuilding of a previously-existing room. This principle has been called that of alternate development, a principle which would have worked in practice as follows: a farmer in the sixteenth century, achieving wealth through the increased cereal prices current in the latter part of that century, would have used his money to replace his old dwelling and build a new house in the regional style. He would not have worried unduly about re-housing his cattle, and so they would have had to exist in the old (probably timber-framed) cowhouse that was still attached to the house. In a generation or two this also would be rebuilt, and so the cycle would continue until finally one might have an eighteenth-century house, heightened about 1870, and with an early nineteenth-century cowhouse forming its lower end. In other cases the cowhouse is probably no more than a simple addition where none existed before. Whatever the explanation, there is certainly a structural break or 'straight joint' in many late long-houses: indeed, surviving long-houses are more often than not of two main builds. The cowhouses are normally very small in size, frequently smaller than the houses to which they are attached: Dan-y-bwlch, Bwlch Trewyn; Tŷ-llwyd, Llanhilleth, and Cwm-dows, Abercarn, all have cowhouses no longer than 13 feet (4m) internally. The partition, where it exists between this outer room and the passage, is normally of massive oak.

GLAMORGAN

In Glamorgan, likewise, many of the eighty or so long-houses that survive have a byre that is clearly later in date than the hall. Many of them, too, have a separate door for the cattle to enter for it was often impossible for man and beast to enter through the same cross-passage: because they were built across the slope the cowhouse was often at a lower level than the house

Lan, Llandeilo, Dyfed. A 1896 lithograph of the front taken from a photograph now missing. Almost a classic long-house apart from the fact that the feeding-passage does not have a door at the far end. The barn at the end is an addition. Lan was a freehold farm of 21 acres in 1896 on which five cows were kept: the cowhouse has room for ten.

and so there was a step in floor levels. Houses with such 'steps' are particularly common in the uplands north of Pontypridd. The single-build long-house of Gilfach-maen Uchaf, Gelligaer, of early seventeenth-century date, has such a stepped cross-passage. A group in the upper Nedd, Afan and Ogwr valleys, on the other hand, have the byre at the upper end of the building. The best documentary reference of the early

nineteenth century concerning Welsh long-houses refers to those of the Vale of Neath. This is a description by William Weston Young in his *Guide to the Scenery &c. of Glyn-Neath* which he published in 1835 though he had lived in the area since 1797:

Many of the farm houses are constructed in a manner suitable to a pastoral people; one end of the building is

15

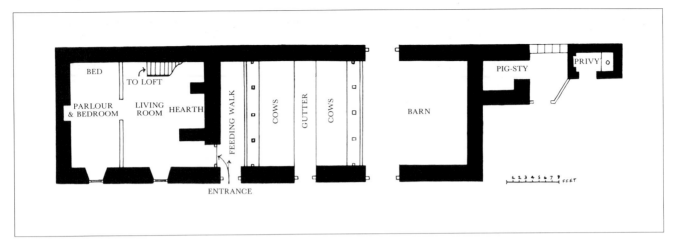

Plan of Lan farmhouse made by I.C. Peate in 1936.

occupied by the family, the other (separated only by a wattle partition) by the cattle, which they inspect during the night. I have many times passed the night in houses of this description and have been much gratified with the order and neatness observed in both divisions.

POWYS

Long-houses, and houses derived from the long-house plan, are also known from Breconshire in south Powys. A major survey of Breconshire houses distinguished three forms: the true long-house, with direct access between house and byre; the false long-house, which comprises a house and byre under one roof but which has lost the direct access between the two parts; and the vestigial long-house, where the house proper resembles the corresponding part of a true or false long-house, but with the byre entirely destroyed or replaced. The 'vestigial long-house', of course, is only the gable-entry house under another name. Together these types comprised the characteristic post-medieval Breconshire farmhouse. Farmhouses which were simply residences and completely divorced from the working activities of the farm made their first certain

appearance in the county in the seventeenth century; the earliest surviving long-houses, on the other hand, appear to have all been of cruck construction, and are therefore probably considerably earlier in date. Indeed, more than one vestigial long-house had a formerly open partition-cruck in its gable, showing that it had once been a longer building.

DYFED

Another concentration of long-houses is in Dyfed in the south-west, and more specifically in the highland areas of north-east Carmarthenshire and mid-Cardiganshire. This particular area was also once characterized by the common use of jointed crucks to support the roof. Jointed crucks are a primitive, though fairly late, version of the cruck truss found so commonly in the rest of Wales and generally in Britain west of the Humber. In this version the truss blades are jointed and pegged to timber uprights seated in the thickness of the wall. Jointed crucks are found in two western areas peripheral to, and exclusive from, the main cruck distribution, namely this part of south-west Wales and part of the south-western peninsula of

England, both areas where trees large enough for full crucks were rare. Their use may be connected with the common occurence of clay walls in both these areas, since a clay wall would not bear the full weight of a normal truss without some reinforcement. The long-house distribution in the south-west is also exactly comparable to the surviving distribution of a further primitive feature, namely wickerwork chimney-hoods.

The long-house tradition in south-west Wales

Many archaic features have persisted longer in south Wales than in the north – the language itself is in many ways more old-fashioned, while several other unrelated distributions point towards the same conclusion: ploughing with oxen continued in the south long after it had declined in the north, while a very primitive form of building, the circular stone pigsty, survives commonly in the south but not at all in the north. The long-house area of the south-west is an even more residual area than the rest of south Wales, as the above features have indicated. It is therefore perhaps not surprising to find that long-houses continued in common use longer in that region than anywhere else in the country.

Some fifty long-houses are known in this group, though that number is undoubtedly only a small percentage of those that once existed. About half of this number are found in the hilly country north of Llandeilo and Llanymddyfri (Llandovery), in the parishes of Llandeilo Fawr, Llangadog, Talyllychau, Llansawel and Llanfihangel Rhos-y-corn. Most of the surviving long-houses in the region appear to be late in date, though that date is generally difficult to establish with any certainty. A date of '1500 odd' apparently existed at Bwlch-gwynt, Llansadwrn, while a truss in the cowhouse at Esgairfynwent, Llanfihangel Rhos-y-corn, bore the more believable date of 1669. Although many long-houses were of quite primitive jointed-cruck construction, it is known that this method of building survived in use until the nineteenth century in south-west Wales. Indeed, the jointed-cruck long-house at Llwyncelyn, Talyllychau (Talley), bears a date of 1739 over the door into the house from the byre.

A detailed description of this group was penned by D. Lleufer Thomas in 1896. The late nineteenth century had seen considerable agitation over the question of land in Wales – landownership, tithe payments, and unwillingness of landlords to provide better buildings on their farms in a period of agricultural depression all created major problems. As a result, a Royal Commission chaired by the Earl Carrington was established in 1893 to inquire into these and allied problems. This Commission, known as the Royal Commission on Land in Wales and Monmouthshire, held numerous sittings throughout Wales between 1893 and 1895. The evidence of these sessions was published in five volumes between 1894 and 1896, whilst the report itself and two volumes of appendices were published in 1896. The Secretary of the Commission was a thirty-year old barrister, Daniel Lleufer Thomas, who had been born on the small farm of Llethr Enoch in the parish of Llandeilo. He had already served as an Assistant Commissioner working on the *Report on the Agricultural Labourer in Wales* and it was he who largely wrote the report of the Land Commission and also prepared a Digest of its contents: the appendices were also his work.

Lleufer Thomas was clearly interested in the traditional architecture of Wales, and in the concept of a 'tribal' or early medieval house, vestiges of which he thought still existed. 'The type', he wrote, 'appears to have survived longest in the northern parts of Carmarthenshire, in the upper region lying between the valleys of the Towy and Teivy, which is, moreover, a district where there is little or no trace of Norman influences.':

We therefore instructed a local architect and surveyor (Mr David Jenkins, FRIBA, of Llandeilo) to prepare for our use a certain number of plans, and to have photographs taken of several of the older farmhouses in the parishes of Llandeilo fawr and Llansadwrn, and from a study of these we are able to see pretty clearly what are the different stages through which the domestic architecture of at least that part of Wales was developed. Practically all the old farmhouses were built in oblong blocks, the dwelling itself being at one end of the block, and separated from the outbuildings by a covered passage. This passage, which, in this part of the country, goes by the

Welsh name of Penllawr, *serves the purpose of a feeding-walk for the cattle, while out of it, on the opposite side, another door opens into the dwelling, being, in fact, the only entrance to it. This door opens into a large general living room, invariably* known as y gegin (*'the kitchen'*), *and there is reason to believe that, at first, this was the only room on the ground floor, but that subsequently a portion of it (being that furthest removed from the entrance) was partitioned off so as to serve*

Blaenwaun, Llansadwrn, Dyfed. A 1896 lithograph of the front taken from a photograph now missing. The house appears to be coloured pink or ochre and the cowhouse white. A change in the roofline suggests that the cowhouse is of later build. The far end of the feeding-passage has been partitioned to form a dairy but the window lighting it could mark the former site of a door. The farm was of 35 acres in 1896 and maintained six cows, three other cattle and a horse.

19

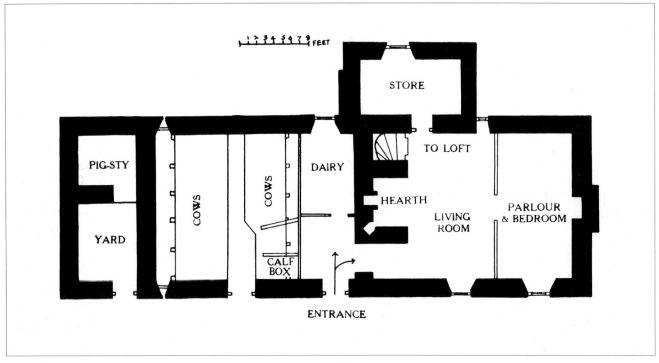

Plan of Blaenwaun farmhouse drawn by I.C. Peate in 1936.

the double purpose of a parlour and a bedroom. This is generally known as y parlwr ('the parlour'), but has sometimes the alternative name of penucha or penisa ('the upper end' or 'lower end'), according to the situation of the house … In the oldest houses, of which we are now speaking, there is seldom more than one fireplace, which is, of course, in the kitchen or large general family room. The extreme end of the feeding-walk, beyond the point where the door opens into the dwelling room, has also, in some cases, been converted into a dairy, but in other cases a lean-to has been built for that purpose.

Over the dwelling there is a 'loft' or 'tallat' (in Welsh, towlod, from the Latin tablatum), approached in some instances by a staircase from without, in which case there is also an aperture in the boarded flooring, underneath which a removable ladder is placed. In other instances the approach to the loft is by means of a proper staircase. In all the older houses the loft was always an attic, and its shape and dimensions can best be realized by saying that it resembled a triangle, formed of the two slanting sides of the roof with the flooring as its base. In other words, the floor of the loft would be generally on a level with the wall-plate. There are, therefore, no windows in this upper storey, except in the gable end.

The roof is set on with 'couples' (W. cyplau), resting on the wall-plate, and on the rafters (W. ceibrenau) are laid rough boughs and twigs as a lower layer, on which is again placed another layer of rushes, heather, or fern, which in turn is covered by a proper thatch of straw. There is no manner of ceiling. The whole of the loft forms one long dormitory, being the sleeping place of the female servants and the children of the house, while at an earlier date, the farmer and wife probably slept in it too. Room is also found in it in many instances for storing cheese, wool and corn.

The walls of the house are usually of very great thickness;

Nant-y-ffin, Llandeilo, Dyfed. A 1896 lithograph of the house taken from a photograph now missing. An unusually lengthy house with later byre, the small sizes of the windows suggesting an early date. Nant-y-ffin was a large farm of 120 acres in 1896, with thirteen or fourteen cows and four or five horses.

there are no windows looking out on the back of the house, but they all face the same way as the entrance, that is, overlooking the farmyard. In fact, as all the windows are small, and as there is no back door, there would be only one entrance to the house, namely, through the feeding-place, and in disturbed times this was probably a great consideration.

These long-houses are generally of a late date, for it is a truism in Welsh vernacular architecture that most pre-Elizabethan houses in the country are to be found east of a line drawn from Rhyl to Newport, while most pre-Hanoverian houses are likewise to be found east of a line from Conwy to Swansea. The general rule is that the further west one travels in Wales, the later in date are the houses. It is therefore not surprising that the long-houses of west Wales are often considerably more than a century later in date than those of Gwent.

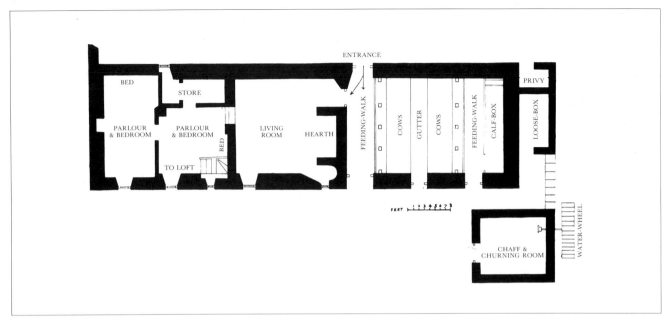

I.C. Peate's plan of Nant-y-ffin farmhouse, 1936. The passage is a true cross-passage.

Three other features implicit in the houses themselves also point to this conclusion.

DATING HOUSES OF THE SOUTH-WEST

Several of these long-houses have a central stair and a central service-room, features which would not commonly be expected in houses of this class much before the eighteenth century. An example of this is Llwyn-celyn, noted above, where there is an area occupied by a formal staircase between the hall and the parlour at the upper end of the house. The same feature is found at, for example, Maesybidiau, Abergorlech, and Cadwgan, Llanfihangel Rhos-y-corn. Such a layout at Pantybetws in the same parish proved recently to have a blocked-up central doorway with the date 1750 above it: this doorway remained in occasional use until the early twentieth century, when it was blocked up. It is unclear whether the dated

doorway was original to the house or a later insertion. A central entry was a frequent late addition to many long-houses. At Lanlas-isaf, Cellan, the central doorway bears above it a tablet inscribed 'BUILT 1772 / REBUILT 1882', when a second storey was added to the house and this doorway made in addition to the existing cross-passage entrance.

The provision of such a second, main, entrance doorway to the house was regarded as a clear sign of social progression. A farmer (or rather, perhaps, a farmer's wife!) with a door provided especially for the house would regard himself (or herself) the clear social superior of an old-fashioned neighbour who still had to enter his living room through the cowhouse. This sense of social differentiation emerges clearly from the following passage, which is a translation of J. Islan Jones's *Yr Hen Amser Gynt*, regarding the parish of Llanfihangel Ystrad, Cardiganshire. The house in question is Pantygwiail, the period about 1890:

It was an old-fashioned house, mostly mud-walled, and

with a thatched roof. Externally, the house and cowhouse looked to be one building, with the door to the house opening first to the cattle's feeding-passage, the bing *in the local dialect, and it was from the* bing *that another door led through the wall of the house into the kitchen. True, there was a 'front door', leading from outside to the parlour or best kitchen, but only persons of a much higher class were ever invited through this front door – the landlord and his family, the steward, the vicar or minister, and suchlike persons ...*

The author then mentions a visit to the house as a child:

When we opened the door, and saw a row of large horns, and below them eyes looking at us in an unfriendly manner, as we thought, we ran out and told our mother that she had shown us the way to the cowhouse and not to the dwelling house.

Canon D. Parry-Jones had a similar experience, as he noted in *Welsh Country Upbringing*, also writing about south Cardiganshire but at a slightly later date:

The cows and the family were housed under one roof, separated by a partition or wall ... [it] is in ruins now and I have only the haziest rememberance of the inner arrangements, but I remember having a bit of a shock when as a boy I opened the door and walked into a cowhouse.

The actual space allocated to the cattle in the cowhouse also suggests a late date for the west Wales examples. At the late-medieval long-house of Black Daren, Llanfeuno, Herefordshire, the evidence of the tethering-posts showed that the cattle were stalled 2 feet 3 inches (70cm) apart. By the time of the reconstruction of Cilewent in 1734, the cattle were allocated a width of 2 feet 6 inches (76cm). The increasing size of livestock during the late eighteenth century and the nineteenth century, due to the introduction of better food-stuffs and higher standards of care, meant that cattle were generally allocated a width of 3 feet (91cm) by the late nineteenth century. This is the space given to the cattle in the byres of these Carmarthenshire and Cardiganshire long-houses, showing that the internal arrangements of these cowhouses, at least, are fairly modern.

The final feature which suggests that these long-

Exterior view of Pant-y-betws, Llanfihangel Rhos-y-corn, Dyfed, in the 1930s. This long-house is classically arranged down the slope. A blocked central doorway was revealed in the 1980s but for a long time the only access to the house was through the cross passage. The house has now been re-thatched.

houses are late in date is the size and form of the cowhouses. We have already noted that the byres of long-houses in eastern Wales, generally of seventeenth-century date, were small and could have housed only a small number of cattle, those cattle in turn entering the cowhouse through the cross-passage. The byres of the south-west group of long-houses are very much larger in size and could often hold a dozen cattle. They also invariably have an entrance in the side wall,

Interior view of Pant-y-betws, 1930s.

and sometimes in the gable also, through which the cattle entered the building: the cross-passage, because of its quite narrow width (5 feet or 1.5m is the average) is used only as a feeding-walk. As in Glamorgan, because of the cross-slope location of these buildings, there is frequently a considerable difference in level between the passage and the cowhouse floor, thus making it impossible in most cases for the cattle ever to have entered through the passage even were it wide enough for them do do so. To understand the implication of a large cowhouse in this context we should consider briefly the tradition of cow-housing in Wales.

In the late nineteenth and early twentieth century, *Calan Gaeaf* (1 November) was a traditional date for putting in the cattle while *Diolchgarwch* (Thanksgiving) the third Monday in October, was another traditional date. In the Aberystwyth region of Cardiganshire, the cattle were normally put in on *Calan Gaeaf*, but if it was a wet season, on 9 October. What was considered important was that they be put in with their backs dry, otherwise ticks would breed. In Carmarthenshire, the cows were tied up at night for the first time on the eve of *Calan Gaeaf*, and normally let loose again on *Ffair John Brown*, 15 April. In south Cardiganshire, the cattle were put in on *Ffair Gynon ddu* – the second Thursday after 15 October. How far back these nineteenth-century dates for wintering the cattle can be carried is a question that cannot at present be answered, for it was only during the first half of the century that all the cattle in the region began to be housed. That certainly was not the case in 1794 when Thomas Lloyd and Charles Hassall wrote their reports for the Board of Agriculture on the condition of agriculture in south-west Wales: Lloyd in his *General View of the Agriculture ... of Cardigan* noted that 'The working cattle [i.e. oxen] are housed in the night. Cows, young cattle and horses are kept out day and night'. Hassall used the same phrase in both his reports, for Pembrokeshire and Carmarthenshire: 'The outdoor stock of cattle are permitted to ramble at large during winter, over the whole farm'. It is thus clear that by no means all the cattle were housed in south-west Wales before the nineteenth century, whereas by the time of the 1896 Land Commission Report it is clear that every animal that could be housed was indeed kept in over the winter.

Since this situation is likely to have existed before the eighteenth century, it is clear why the seventeenth-century byres in the long-houses of Gwent should be small and those in the south-west much larger: the latter are designed to accommodate all the cattle kept and are thus later in date, most probably of the late eighteenth or even the nineteenth centuries. The fact that the cattle did not enter the cowhouse through the cross-passage in these western examples is further evidence of the progression away from the primitive long-house recorded by Weston Young a century earlier.

The evolution of the Welsh farmhouse

For several centuries, the long-house and its allied plan-forms remained one of the most important types of farmhouse in Wales. This was the case in south-east Wales from the late sixteenth century (at least) until the eighteenth or nineteenth centuries, and in great areas of west Wales from the seventeenth century to the late nineteenth century. The gable-entry farmhouses of the south-east that were separate from their farm buildings may also have been derived from an ancestral long-house form: this is certainly possible typologically. A typical British farmhouse is often several centuries older than its associated farm buildings, which were not considered so important and so were not built in a permanent form as early. Bearing this in mind, it is the single-build long-house which is worthy of comment, rather than one showing two periods of construction. In addition, the trend in Britain for many centuries has been to separate the farm buildings from the house, a trend which still

Coedlannau, Pencader, Dyfed. A 1930s photograph showing house and cowhouse. The varying texture of the masonry in the front wall of the house suggests that it was originally single-storey and raised in the early years of this century.

continues. It is therefore difficult to conceive of a long-house as being originally a gable-entry dwelling house, with a cowhouse located elsewhere on the farmyard, the house at a later period having a byre added to it. On the other hand, a gable-entry house originally built as a long-house and later shorn of its byre, or having its byre converted to a kitchen or parlour, is perfectly feasible if this thesis of the gradual separation of the functions of the house and the farm is accepted. The appearance of non-gable-entry plans in much of Wales in the seventeenth century, in addition, would militate against the continued existence of long-houses in those areas. Only isolated examples would survive outside the gable-entry province of the south-east, those isolated examples themselves reflecting the occasional occurrence of untypical houses outside their own culture-provinces.

By the early eighteenth century farmhouses of a more formal appearance with Renaissance-derived or 'Georgian' plans were being introduced into the Welsh countryside. The traditional regional plans were replaced, and after about 1730 very few houses were built following the old plans. Farmhouses were henceforth roughly symmetrical about a central stair-passage, and had windows regularly placed about the central doorway. The chimney-stacks were moved to the gables even in those areas such as mid-Wales where they had traditionally been clustered in the centre of the buildings. Whatever the true story of the evolution of the Welsh long-house, it remains a fact that hundreds and possibly thousands of dwellings with the humans at one end and the cattle at the other were found from the late sixteenth or early seventeenth century, principally in south Wales. The earliest surviving examples are from the south-east border county, and one recent theory sees it as significant that this was an area where cattle raiding and rustling was endemic at that time. The long-house, with its single range, thick walls and easily-secured cross-passage could thus be seen as an architectural response to the disturbed conditions of the Welsh Marches, offering an added degree of security against cattle thieves. However, long-houses continued in use in west Wales until the twentieth century, with the direct central door into the house being ignored in favour of the old

Whithen, Pencader, Dyfed. A 1930s photograph of the front and cross-passage entrance, with evidence of rebuilding near the passage. The roof was originally thatched. Notice the cobbled walkway in front of the buildings.

feeding-passage entry. The most interesting fact about the Welsh long-house, perhaps, lies not so much in its dark and tangled origins but in the fact that so many farming families found it ideal for their needs over several centuries, as indeed did the inhabitants of Cilewent for so many years.

The long-house of Cilewent

The farm of Cilewent lay at a height of 1,050 feet (306m) above sea level near the headwaters of the river Claerwen in the large upland parish of Llansanffraid Cwmteuddwr, six miles (10km) south-west of Rhaeadr in the historical county of Radnorshire and the modern county of Powys. The name refers to the home, retreat or sanctuary (*cil*) of a person called Ewent. The form *Ciloerwynt* ('shelter from the cold wind') seen on some maps is a fanciful invention of the last century. Very little is known of the early history of the house. We shall see later that it was built in about 1470, when all of Llansanffraid Cwmteuddwr formed part of the lands of the Cistercian abbey of Strata Florida. Strata Florida owned more land than any other religious establishment in Wales, and its granges of Pennardd, Blaenaeron, Mefenydd, Cwmteuddwr and Cwmystwyth lay in a great block across mid-Wales, measuring nearly twenty miles from west and east and fifteen miles from north to south. Cwmteuddwr grange was a large area of common pasture with isolated holdings paying rent to the abbey. In the early sixteenth century it was supervised by a monk-bailiff, John York, who continued in his post after the suppression of the monasteries in 1536 when Strata Florida was annexed by the Crown and became royal property.

The first known mention of Cilewent occurs in 1568. Cwmteuddwr grange had then been granted to Sir Richard Devereux who leased parts of it to Michael Sewell, gentleman of Gloucestershire. On 1 December 1568 Sewell and his wife Joan sub-leased the tenement of *Kele Gwent* to Meredith ap Edward, gentleman, of Llansanffraid, and Edward ap Rice ap Meredith, for a period of twenty-one years at a rent of 13*s* 4*d* a year. The lease was not run its full course, however, and Edward ap Rhys (as his name would be spelt today)

soon had a new landlord. On 29 April of that year Queen Elizabeth gave to Robert and Thomas Warecoppe:

…all that mesuage landes teñtes [tenements] *& hereditaments with thapp' teñces* [with their appurtenances] *set leinge & beinge in Cumytoithur in ye countie of Radnor comonlie called & knowen by the name of Keelewent with all landes teñtes meadows lesowes pastures woods feadinges heathes and comon sufficient in their wastes of Comotoithor marisies belonginge or app'taininge to ye sayd landes & teñtes or to any of them wch sometime were p'cell* [parcel] *of the possesiones of ye late dissolved monostery of Strata florida …*

The next day, they in turn transferred the land to Sir James Croft and Thomas Wigmore. Croft was Controller or her Majesty's Household and a Privy Counsellor, and Wigmore a gentleman of Shobdon, Herefordshire. They rented the land to Edward ap Rees of Llansanffraid for 2*s*. to be paid in even portions on the feasts of the Annunciation and of St Michael.

Edward ap Rees was also to pay suit to Sir James's mill: he was not allowed to take his corn to be ground at any other mill. If these conditions were not met Croft could reclaim the land until the money was forthcoming. In addition, 'ye said Edward ap Rees & his heires shall paye or cause to be payed to ye sayd James Crofte Knight or his heires the best beaste or fortie shillings in ye name of an herryot at the deceasse of any tenannte …' Two years later, on 10 October 1579, this agreement came to an end and Croft and Wigmore sold Cilewent outright to Edward ap Rees 'in consideracõn of the some [sum] of thirtie five poundes of good & leffulle [lawful] money of England to be well & trulie payd …'. Edward ap Rees is described as 'yeoman'. The document was witnessed by David Williams, Richard Aubrey, Ieuan Lloyd and David Roberts. The document is endorsed 'Evan Pugh's ffeeffarme for ye Tenemt called Kilewent. Charged with 2*s*. Chief Rent'.

No other surviving document of this period mentions either Cilewent or Edward ap Rees, but three wills indicate the nature of the parish's economy at this time. Thomas ap Ieuan Llewellyn's will of

Cilewent in its original location, 1954. A later cowhouse and hay-barn are found at the upper end.

January 1577 listed his possessions as two oxen worth 40s. (£2); six cattle worth £6; three heifers, 30s.; two mares, 40s.; six sheep, 12s.; ten goats, 10s.; household stuff, 20s.; and debts due to him 30s. Howell ap Owen, yeoman (1578) was wealthier: he had thirty cattle, £20; two oxen and nine bullocks, £6.6s.8d.; two yearling bullocks, 13s.4d.; five heifers, 33s.4d.; ten calves, 20s.; 128 sheep, £12; twelve goats, 12s.; four pigs, 2s.; horse and mare, 33s.4d.; household stuff worth 26s.8d.;

mortgage money on lands, £10; and debts due to him £6.2s.10d., a total of £60.10s.2d. Edward ap David's will was proved in the same year: he left five cattle, five calves and a heifer, all worth £3.6s.8d.; two bullocks, 20s.; six sheep and eight lambs, 13s.; household stuff, 20s.; and about five acres of oats in the fields, worth 10s. It is likely that Edward ap Rees's estate would have been similar, but unfortunately, his will has not survived amongst other Archdeaconry of Brecon wills.

DATING THE BUILDING

Edward ap Rees would have had difficulty in recognizing the house that stands in the Welsh Folk Museum today. This is not because of any inaccuracy in the way the building was re-erected; rather, it was because the house was drastically altered in the eighteenth century. The only parts of the house that are earlier than this date are the two cruck trusses in the cowhouse end (the large roof trusses in the form of the letter A that rise from the walls and meet at the apex of the roof) and some of the large timbers associated with them. An attempt was made to date these crucks in 1990 using the modern scientific technique of dendrochronology or tree-ring dating.

Seven sample cores of timber were taken from the two crucks and one of the purlins associated with them and dated at the University of Nottingham's Tree-Ring Dating Laboratory. Tree-ring dating works on the principle that each year an oak tree (the commonest timber used in traditional building) grows an extra thickness or ring immediately under the bark. This growth varies from year to year according to weather conditions, with wide rings being produced in good seasons and narrow rings in poor years. Over a period of time a sequence of rings is formed whose pattern can be compared to that from other trees from the same or indeed a different area. A master sequence of ring widths, representing the average widths of rings, can then be formed from timber from a series of buildings. Such master sequences or chronologies for oak have been formed, for example, for Ireland, the south of England and the West Midlands, and samples from areas with no sound existing tree-ring chronology such as Wales can sometimes be cross-matched with these existing chronologies.

The date obtained from cross-matching a building in this way is the date of the last ring on the sample core. At least sixty rings must be present. If bark is present then the felling date is known, and as timber in the past was almost invariably used in its green or unseasoned state, the date of building is also known. It is also possible to give a good indication of date if the thirty or so outer rings, known as the sapwood, are present. Five of the seven samples from Cilewent could

The re-erection of Cilewent at the Welsh Folk Museum, 1957. The picture is taken from the house end looking towards the cowhouse. The different forms of the two pairs of crucks is noticeable.

be formed into a single sequence of 120 rings, ending with complete sapwood on a purlin. It is clear that the two blades of both crucks each came from the same tree, and that the two or three trees used all grew at a single site for they had clearly experienced the same growing conditions and weather patterns. The sequence produced a reasonable match with known chronologies at two points in the late fifteenth century. On the earlier dating, the trees grew from 1339 until they were felled between September 1459 and April 1460, and on the later dating they grew from 1356 until felled between September 1476 and April 1477. It therefore seems that the two crucks and the purlins associated with them were made over the winters of either 1460 or 1477: it is impossible to choose between these two dates at the moment. The

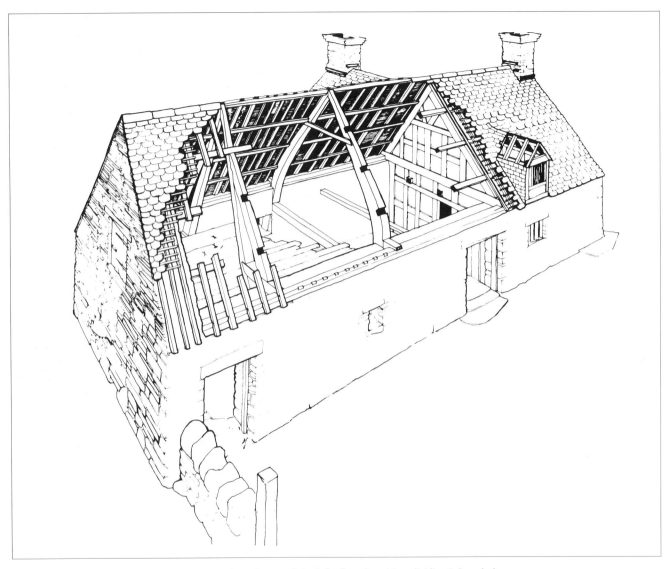

Cutaway drawing of Cilewent, showing the crucks in the cowhouse and the timber-framed partitions dividing it from the house.

fact that the purlins are of the same date as the crucks also suggests that the trusses have not been re-used from another building, and that Cilewent indeed dates from the late fifteenth century.

The cruck blades are fully bedded into the stone wall so it is impossible to study their faces. The building was dismantled and re-erected some thirty-five years ago and no detailed notes survive. Nevertheless, it is

30

Exterior of Cilewent in its original location, 1956.

probable that the two cruck blades would have supported a timber-framed structure rather than the present stone building. The original Cilewent, of which these two crucks are the survivors, may well have looked like Hendre'r-ywydd Uchaf from Llangynhafal in Clwyd, also re-erected at St Fagans and itself dated to 1508. The gable or pine-end crucks could have become exposed to the weather and been replaced at the same time as the side walls. Very many cruck buildings are known to have been treated in this fashion for it was possible to replace the walls without seriously disturbing the roof. The Hendre-wen barn from Llanrwst, also in the Welsh Folk Museum, is a case in point, with its original timber-framed walls replaced by stone about 1800. Stone walls would have been a most unusual feature in a fifteenth-century

The fireplace in the dairy, before removal. Notice the white-washed walls and the wooden racks hanging from the ceiling.

farm in mid-Wales. However, timber-framed buildings are still common on the lowlands within a few miles of Cilewent's original site.

THE REBUILDING OF CILEWENT

By the early eighteenth century, fashion and climate had conspired together to radically alter the appearance of the house, now over 250 years old. Timber-framed buildings like Cilewent were considered to be old-fashioned, while the heavy rain and penetrating winds of its exposed location would have resulted in considerable decay to the walls. Similar rebuilding was going on all over the Welsh moorlands. It seems likely that Cilewent's original timber walls were replaced by stone in 1734, which is the date carved on the head-beam above the main doorway. The beam also bears two sets of initials, S.P.E. and E.E.H. Such inscriptions do not always refer to dates of building or rebuilding – they may commemorate marriages or similar significant family events – but in this case the former seems likely. The bearers of these initials have not yet been identified, and indeed little is known of the families who lived in Cilewent until the nineteenth century.

Many farmhouses were certainly being built or rebuilt in the 1730s in Wales, as other date-inscriptions attest. In England, surviving inscriptions look like a pyramid when plotted on a graph, rising from some ten inscriptions in the 1550s, peaking sharply at nearly 300 in the 1690s and plummetting rapidly thereafter to some 120 by the 1740s. The pattern in Wales is quite different. Building was obviously dependent on the availability of ready money; the Welsh economy, with its greater emphasis on rearing cattle and sheep than on growing corn, resulted in different patterns of wealth from England. Welsh date-inscriptions reach a first peak in the 1630s, with some seventy-seven examples. As in England, the 1640s were a decade of civil war and little building, but prosperity was soon regained and there was a further peak of activity in the 1670s. This was followed by a slump until the years following 1710 and a further peak in the 1730s, slumping again in the 1740s. Such date-inscriptions are much more commonly found on north Wales houses rather than ones from south Wales, but Radnorshire enjoyed quiet activity from the 1630s on. Cilewent's date of 1734 is entirely consistent with this pattern.

The rebuilt house was L-shaped in plan, some 56 feet (17m) long along its front. It was constructed of local shaly rubble; there was no need for foundations for the walls sat directly on the living rock which outcropped in the yard. There were two doors. One hard by the lower gable led into the stable which was delineated internally by the line of one of the cruck trusses. Beyond the stable lay a cowhouse where two rows of cattle could be stalled back-to-back across the building. The cattle entered the building through the main doorway, which also led to the living house. Between these two areas was a passage which in most long-houses has a door at the far end also; this did not. This passage, at 5 feet 11 inches (1.8m), was wide enough to accommodate the cattle entering it and turning into the byre.

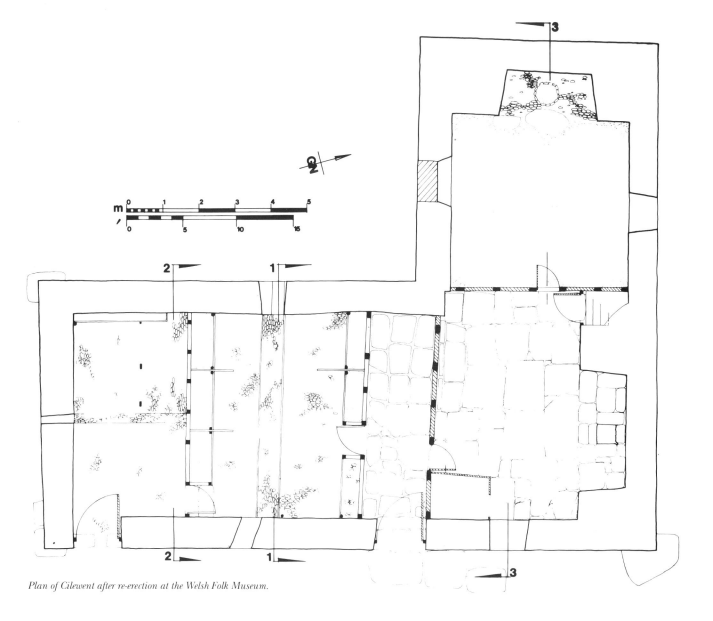

Plan of Cilewent after re-erection at the Welsh Folk Museum.

A full-height timber-framed partition separated the passage from the family quarters, which consisted of one room in the main part of the house and one in the base of the L. The first room was the main living room of the house. Like the passage, it was floored with large rough slabs of shale. The fireplace faced the door, in the thickness of the gable. A stone staircase by its side led to the two upstairs rooms. The small boarded area near the single wooden-mullioned glass-less window is probably later: it served as a pantry. A

The main fireplace in Cilewent, as furnished at the Welsh Folk Museum.

further timber-framed partition separated this room from another, square room beyond. This was originally cross-lit by two windows (one was blocked in later and turned into open shelves) and had a large fireplace. The floor was of earth. It presumably functioned as a dairy – a fire was required for making cheese – and as an extra work-room where a second fireplace was always useful for boiling clothes and animal feed.

Cilewent in its rebuilt state was a form of long-house, a type of farmhouse whereby humans and animals lived under one roof and in which there was internal access between the two parts. Cilewent is not a typical long-house, however: it differs from the usual form in two important details. Firstly, the passage between the house and cowhouse normally has a door at the far end and is a true cross-passage; nevertheless, many otherwise usual long-houses lack this feature. The second difference is more distinctive. Long-houses almost invariably have the fireplace backing on to this passage so that entry to the house-part is past the side of the chimney-breast. Here, the fireplace is in the upper gable, a major deviation from the normal pattern. How does Cilewent compare with local long-houses? In Radnorshire only ten of the known cruck houses have a cowhouse attached to them, and in all but three the intercommunication was blocked in recent times. Indeed, only Cilewent, Gelli Cadwgan in Llanfaredd, and Celyn, Llansteffan, can be said with certainty to have contemporary byres, although the nearby Llannerch y Cawr (which is in Breconshire) is of one build with house and byre constructed at the same date. A chimney backing on to the entry is the usual pattern for the area, though a number of L-shaped examples are known.

EIGHTEENTH-CENTURY LIFE AT CILEWENT

The house afforded little privacy for its inhabitants. Apart from the family, a female servant would almost certainly have been employed to help with the dairying and the lighter farm tasks, and depending on the age of sons, there was usually work for a male servant as well. He would have been expected to sleep in the loft above the animals, but all would have spent their evening in the single living-room. This was not a living-room as we would know it; rather, it was also the kitchen and a work-room where many of the domestic activities of the household were carried out. All cooking was done on the open hearth in the huge inglenook fireplace. The fire was never allowed to go out, and the ashes in the pit or *uffern* ('hell') underneath served as a heat reservoir until they were finally taken out to be turned into soap. Most of the food was based on either milk or oatmeal or both: the baking-oven built under the stairs is probably a later insertion. The existing stone oven is a modern replacement of a north Devon clay oven which could not be rebuilt. Such clay ovens were common in farmhouses in south and mid Wales and were imported by sea from the seventeenth century

onwards. This example probably dated to the nineteenth century.

The layout of the lower end provides vital clues to the nature of the economy in the eighteenth century. The tethering posts show that the cattle were stalled in pairs. Six cattle were housed in a row facing into the stable, and a similar number facing back into the passage they had used to enter the byre. One end of

The remains of the North Devon clay oven in the main fireplace, shown during the dismantling of the building.

The interior of the cowhouse, before removal.

The interior of the cowhouse, after re-erection and looking through into the house.

this area is now divided for use as a calf-pen. If this is original, then a total of ten animals were housed in the byre; if later, then a dozen. These cattle were probably the ancestors of our modern Welsh Blacks: each was given a width of only 2 feet 6 inches (70cm) and it is known that the average weight of such a beast in 1710 was only 370 lb. (168kg). We do not know if these twelve were the total number of cattle kept at Cilewent, but it is likely that the milking cattle, at least, would have been housed here. Twelve beasts compares well with the two oxen, six cattle and three heifers owned by Thomas ap Ieuan Llewellyn in 1577 and the five cattle, one heifer, two bullocks and five calves of Edward ap David. That these farmers died some 150 years before Cilewent was rebuilt is of no consequence, for the house was rebuilt around the existing crucks and so could not be made wider: with the cattle stalled in this fashion, no more could be accommodated than in the old house unless the cowhouse end was made longer.

The stable contained room for two horses, tied individually and separated by a partition to prevent them kicking each other. It was normal in eighteenth-century Radnorshire to use a mixed team of two oxen led by two horses for ploughing, though horses were generally more useful as draught animals and certainly would have fared better in any capacity on Cilewent's steep land than oxen would have. When acquired by the Welsh Folk Museum, the house was surrounded by sheep pens. They probably replace earlier ones on the same site, and certainly the importance of sheep is underlined by the large size of the yard, which must have been used for gathering the flock prior to washing and shearing. The sheep would have grazed the commons surrounding the farm, where also peat would have been cut in summer to serve as fuel. A considerable amount of peat would have been required to serve the needs of the family throughout the year, and great stacks of it would have been kept near the house. The little stone shed facing the house may have been used to store dried peat ready for use.

The common grazings would have served to feed the sheep flocks around the year, but the horses and cattle required hay which would have been grown on the flat

A view from the house into the cowhouse, 1954.

lands immediately around the house. The family itself required a considerable supply of oatmeal, the staple basis of the diet of upland Wales. Therefore oats would have been grown, and the straw would have been used as bedding for the animals: bracken was also cut for this purpose. Straw and hay alike would have been stored in the capacious loft above the stable and byre. The large ark chest in the passage was a ubiquitous article of furniture in such farms: in it the oatmeal was stored, packed down tightly by having the younger members of the family wear clean white stockings and tread it down. The detachable lid would be turned upside down and, with two poles under it, serve as a hand-barrow. Wheeled vehicles or implements would have been unknown: sleds (*ceir llusg*), would have been used to take manure out to the fields and gather the crops.

There was a locally held belief that cattle would give more milk if they could see the flames of the fire, as indeed some of the Cilewent cattle could. That milk was used for making butter and particularly cheese, as no doubt also was ewes' milk. Making butter and cheese, along with rearing cattle to be entrusted to drovers who would walk them to the English markets, were some of the corner-stones of the Welsh rural economy at this time. The large size of the dairy at Cilewent, with its cheese-press and storage rack, graphically illustrates this. Another corner-stone, particularly important to mid-Wales, was the sale of wool to the great woollen industry centred around Newtown and the Severn valley. Considerable use was made of the wool at home, too, and spinning and knitting stockings was an important winter activity in isolated farms such as this.

NINETEENTH-CENTURY HUSBANDRY

This much can be gleaned about the economy of Cilewent in the early to mid-eighteenth century from an examination of the house. The account of Radnorshire given by Samuel Lewis in his *Topographical Dictionary of Wales* (1833) gives considerable information about the situation in the early nineteenth century. The parish of Llansanffraid Cwmteuddwr then had 867 inhabitants. 'Of the whole of this extensive tract', Lewis wrote, 'a very inconsiderable portion only is under cultivation; the remainder, being chiefly mountainous, affords excellent pasturage to numerous flocks of sheep and herds of cattle, which are reared for the English markets.' Slate quarries were worked, and lead had been discovered in Cwm Elan in 1796. Most of the parish was open mountain, with the farms limited to the valley floors around the Claerwen and its tributary the Elan. Indeed, noted Lewis, much of the county of Radnor was in a similar condition:

Of the superficial area of the county, about one-third is supposed to be enclosed and of this enclosed portion not more than a fourth part is under the plough at the same time. In the vicinity of market-towns, and on farms where the soil is good, the cultivation of grain for sale prevails to a considerable extent: but, as regards the whole of the county, it must be observed, that the distance from large corn markets, the high price of lime, and the roughness and moisture of the climate, operate as great discouragements to the growth of grain; and the chief object of the farmers is to grow only what is sufficient for their own consumption, viewing their stock of sheep, cattle, and horses as the main sources of their profit. It is a common practice to plough a piece of sward (which is sometimes pared and burnt for a crop of wheat), and to take, in the first instance, one or two crops of oats; then to summer fallow the land, giving it all the manure of the farm, and what lime can be procured, for a crop of wheat: after this the land is generally thought capable of bearing a crop of barley, with which the better sort of farmers sow clover and grass seeds; the crop is mown the first year, and afterwards the land is suffered to rest, whilst some other portion of the farm undergoes the same process. Rye and a mixture of rye and wheat (called Monk's corn) were formerly much grown, but are now seldom seen. Potatoes, as a field crop, are extensively and successfully cultivated: peas, though precarious and unprofitable, are sometimes sown; and flax, for domestic purposes, rather than for sale. In the mode of cultivation there is little that is peculiar; the implements are cheap and imperfect, though much improved. A light cart, drawn by three small stout horses, is in general use: waggons also are common. A ground sledge, with two wheels in front, is found useful in drawing heavy weights down steep declivities; and a rude car without any wheels is still used for conveying peat from the mountains. The ploughs in general use have a bent iron mould-board, similar to those in Herefordshire; but the Scotch plough, drawn by two horses abreast, is gradually advancing into use throughout the county.

Such land as cannot be irrigated, and which may be also either too steep and rugged, or at too great a distance from the farm-yard, to be advantageously ploughed, is usually devoted to the pasturage of cattle and horses, both of which are reared in considerable numbers. The black cattle, which still prevail in the adjoining county of Cardigan, have not for many years been much bred in Radnorshire: they gave place to a coarse hardy variety of the long-horned breed, introduced from Shropshire, which were generally of a brindled colour, and gave much milk: some of these still remain but they have in a great measure been superseded by the Herefordshire breed, which, being found to be sufficiently hardy to endure the scanty food and rough climate, have the advantage of growing to a larger size, and possess a greater aptitude to

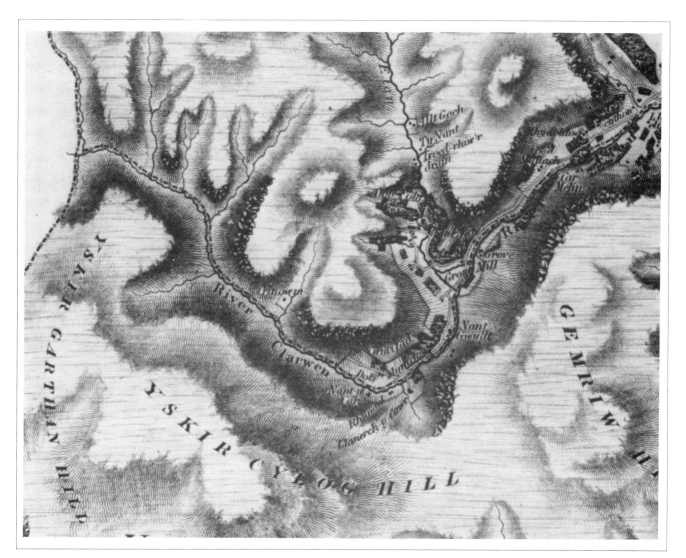

The map of Glamorgan, Brecknock and Radnor by Greenwood, 1828, showing Cilewent as Crinowin *located by the banks of the river Claerwen in the lower left-hand corner.*

Cilewent in its setting, 1954.

fatten. The draught horse in general use is small and ill-shaped, but capable of enduring great fatigue. The original Welsh ponies are still bred in the mountains, and their price in the markets has of late years increased: of their activity, courage, and patience, and of their strength as compared with their size and the little sustenance they require, it is difficult to dilate in terms too favourable. Where so large a

portion of the surface is unenclosed, the pasturage of the commons necessarily forms an object of interest to the farmers: on the lower ranges of commons the young cattle on the farm, of every kind, are frequently depastured; but for the most part cattle are found to require more attendance and care than can well be afforded them on commons. Throughout the entire county the breeding of sheep is the primary object of the

A family group posed at Cilewent, taken from a framed print of about 1899. The members are John Scott (a visitor); Elizabeth Jones and her brother Evan; their grandmother Mary Williams; their mother Margaret Jones; and a brother, Thomas.

farmers adjoining the open lands. On the western side of it a small active breed prevails, mostly without horns, with white faces and legs, and having long, open, coarse wool, abounding with kemps. But in the forest of Radnor, and on the lower hills on the north and south of that elevated range, a breed has been produced by the introduction of rams from Shropshire: these sheep are well covered with a fleece of thick close wool, and have larger carcases than those just described: they are, however, much less hardy, and can only be maintained by farmers who can afford some shelter to their stock during the winter. Throughout the county it is the practice to take the ewes into the enclosed grounds in October, and, if possible, the lambs of the preceding spring also: the wether sheep, for the most part, brave the climate of the hills during the whole of the year. These sheep, when fat, usually weigh from nine to fourteen lb. per quarter; and their fleeces average from two to three lb.: vast numbers of them are annually driven into Essex and Hertfordshire, where the superior quality of the mutton ensures for them a ready sale. Large quantities of butter are still made in the county, though it is chiefly an object to the smaller farmers: it is salted during the summer, and placed with great care and cleanliness in tubs, in which it was thus formerly carried to the fairs in Herefordshire: this article of produce, however, has of late years been sold by the farmers at their own houses. Oxen, which were formerly much used in husbandry are now sold at too early an age to be so employed, and almost the whole draught of the county is now executed by horses. In a county of which nearly two-thirds are unenclosed it may be presumed that there exists great capability of improvement, and the large tracts of low commons which are seen on passing through the centre of it tend to confirm this idea. Of late years, considerable encroachments have been made on the wastes both by cottagers and by farmers, and even this lawless process has tended somewhat to improve the lands taken in. About six parishes have been submitted to the operation of enclosure acts, but the expense which attends the allotment of the land, and the still greater cost of maintaining the fences, discourage any further attempts of this sort: from one of these attempts, indeed, in the immediate vicinity of Rhaiadr [sic], the most beneficial effects have resulted, the produce of a small common having been increased many hundredfold, to the great advantage of the inhabitants of that town. Many tracts still remain which are susceptible of almost equal improvement; but the rough surface of the pasture land throughout the greater part of the county, overgrown as it is, in many parts, with rushes, shews that, without an extensive and effectual system of drainage, the soil can never be brought to its utmost point of fertility. It is by this, rather than any other, mode that the improvement of the low lands can be effected. On the hills the use of iron wire in fencing has been introduced to some extent, and is likely to enable the farmers to defend their lands from the mountain sheep, where no other means would avail.

Cilewent at the time of this description was a farm with six fields of enclosed land totalling 87 acres. The Tithe Map of 1838 shows that it was owned by Elizabeth Price, Jane Jones and Rees Jones. Rees Jones occupied the farm; he also owned a share of the adjoining 159-acre farm of Cwm-coel. The first detailed census came three years later, in 1841. John and Magdalene Jones, aged 70 and 75 respectively, employed four young servants – Evan Jones (15), John Lloyd (10), Gwen Arthur (20) and Mary Price (10). The 1851 census saw only two female servants at home – Mary Rees aged 50 and Elizabeth Williams (12). Thomas Middleton, the head of the household in 1861, was a 24-year-old shepherd; he was assisted by his housekeeper, Jane Pugh aged 26, and a 10-year-old cowman, Thomas Thomas. By 1871 another new family was in place. Evan Jones was a 23-year-old shepherd who had been born in Cardiganshire. He and his wife Margaret had just had their first child when the census took place: by 1881 four more children had arrived to give three sons and two daughters. They employed no servants, though Evan's mother-in-law was visiting when the 1881 census was made. The old lady, Mrs Williams, was visiting again when a family photograph was taken in about 1899! The tranquility and loneliness of life at Cilewent was about to be shattered, however.

By 1890 the city fathers of Birmingham were forced to the conclusion that something drastic had to be done about their water supply. Local reserves were not sufficient for the rapidly growing second city of the United Kingdom, and the nearest viable spot for a supply was considered to be valleys of the Claerwen and the Elan. Rainfall was high – 66 inches (167cm) a year – and the water was soft and very pure. The area contained a population of only about 180 in its seventy square miles. The Bill authorizing the work received Royal assent on 22 June 1892 and the land required was purchased compulsorily. In this way the ownership of Cilewent passed to Birmingham Corporation. Three great dams were built between 1893 and 1904: one that would have stood at Cilewent itself was never built, although the Claerwen Dam of 1951 came close. By 1955 the house was considered too old-fashioned, and the Corporation built a new bungalow for the tenants, donating Cilewent to the Welsh Folk Museum.

Daily work at Cilewent, 1954.

Bibliography

Fox, Sir Cyril and Lord Raglan, *Monmouthshire Houses*,
   I-III, 1951-54.
Peate, Iorwerth C., *The Welsh House*, 3rd. ed., 1946.
Smith, Peter, *Houses of the Welsh Countryside*, 2nd ed.,
   1988.
Thomas, D. Lleufer (ed.). *Report of the Royal Commission
   on Land in Wales and Monmouthshire*, 1896.
Wiliam, Eurwyn, *The Historical Farm Buildings of Wales*,
   1986.

The photographs of the Dyfed long-houses
reproduced in this book were taken for David Jenkins,
the architect from Llandeilo, in 1896, and were given
to I.C. Peate (the first Curator of the Welsh Folk
Museum) by D. Lleufer Thomas, Secretary of the 1896
Royal Commission. They are now in the care of the
Welsh Folk Museum and are reproduced here for the
first time.